Onwards to Organised
A Decluttering Mindset Workbook:
How to start and keep going

First published in 2023
Copyright © Amy Thompson 2023

All rights reserved. No part of this book may be reproduced in any form on by an electronic or mechanical means, including information storage and retrieval systems, without permission in writing from the publisher, except by a reviewer who may quote brief passages in a review.

ISBN 9798363708886

Acknowledgements:

Thank you to all the wonderful APDO members who have inspired me. In particular: Jo Cooke, Tilo Flache, Caroline Rogers, Sarah Bickers, Karen Eyre-White, Juliet Landau-Pope.

To Shona Chambers for excellent ideas and advice.
To Clare Law for endless support and wise words.

To my friends and family for believing in me and my business.

Chirp

Onwards to Organised
A Decluttering Mindset Workbook:
How to start and keep going

    Welcome to Onwards to Organised! It's great to have you here.
Since I set up my professional organising business in 2019, I've had the privilege of being part of many people's decluttering journeys. I've seen incredible demonstrations of resilience and bravery. I've joined clients in their celebration of progress and guided them through moments of despair. I've seen sighs of relief, elated whoops of joy, furrowed brows of worry, and a fair few tears. It's OK to find this hard. It is hard.

    You've come to this point because you are willing to challenge yourself in order to get the life you want, and that's an incredibly brave step. You've decided that enough is enough and that you are ready to make a change. Perhaps you're frozen trying to decide where to start, perhaps you've tried a few times before and found it too overwhelming or perhaps you've made progress before but things have slipped backwards.
I have seen all of these things, and I have also seen people overcome them. I strongly believe that we are all capable of change, it's all about finding the right method for you, and believing in your strength to persevere.

I also speak from personal experience. As a child I was always a collector of objects. I would keep pretty rocks, leaves, postcards, tickets, cute packaging.
I grew up in the 90s when stickers and Pogs were all the rage.
Looking back now I can see that these kinds of fads are actually a sneaky way of teaching children to become consumers, and pressuring parents to buy. In the playground, you were judged to be cool if you had the right clothes, or stickers which were glittery, holographic, puffy, scented, neon.... etc

This resulted in several of these fads being banned at our school, but another always quickly replaced it. The problem wasn't the stickers or Pogs or Pokemon cards. The problem is that as humans living in a capitalist and consumerist society, we are taught to put a disproportionate value on possessing objects.

By indulging these fads we are teaching our children that other people's opinion of them is based on their possessions. On the other hand, by not indulging the fad you are denying the child the currency of the playground. A very difficult choice!

I'm talking about children's fads because it's a much more obvious version of the system we live in as adults. The objects we desire might be different, and we might be more covert in our judgements of others, but ultimately we have all learned from a young age to make judgements based on possessions.

The problem is that you cannot easily escape this system. It exists all around us and the alternative, rejecting capitalism and living completely off grid, is not something easily undertaken. For the majority of us our only option is to find a way to exist within the system without it causing us too much damage, and without causing too much damage to our planet and fellow humans.

As a teenager I was rather lost as to who I wanted to be in the world. I tried on many different versions of myself (which is pretty normal for a teenager) but with each of these re-inventions came the different clothes, accessories, trinkets, books etc. Because I didn't outright reject each of these identities as they came and went, my possessions accumulated.

It was also a time when ebay had just become popular, and being able to buy second-hand clothes for next to nothing was thrilling, as well as the bidding system adding urgency and excitement to purchases.

I had clothes in my wardrobe which belonged to a version of myself which had either ceased to exist, or had never got off the ground in the first place. I had jewellery I never wore, books I never read, shoes I couldn't walk in, and art supplies I never used.

When I was in my early twenties I lost both of my grandparents within the space of a few months, and their home had to be emptied quickly. I was moving out after getting my first job after uni, and I jumped at the chance to inherit a large amount of kitchenware so as to save having to buy it.

It turned out that my grandma had been quite a collector herself, and I received an enormous amount of stuff which I took without much consideration for whether I actually needed it.

I continued in this way throughout my early twenties. Not paying much attention to my relationship with my belongings, shopping for bargains, collecting anything that appealed to me aesthetically, and rarely throwing anything away.

The turning point came after I moved house three times in as many years. There's nothing like moving house to bring you face to face with the amount of stuff you own. Packing things away for the third time, having not used it since I had last unpacked it was pretty confronting.

There wasn't as much awareness of decluttering in the public consciousness as there is now. So with no particular tools or guidance I dived in! My main motivation was not wanting to go through the upheaval of moving so much stuff yet again.

I started by researching where I could send my unwanted items. It felt important to me that they would go to somebody who really needed them, and through some research I found a local women's shelter which was accepting donations of clothing and toiletries directly.

I found it helpful to picture my objects being handed to somebody who had perhaps had to flee their home at short notice bringing very little with them. I found that this image made me more likely to part with an item. Cozy jumpers, little bottles of shampoo, slippers, all these things felt much more valuable to this imagined person than to me.

I remember sitting on my bedroom floor at 10 o'clock at night sorting through my jewellery box, when I suddenly started to think differently.
So many of the things I had kept simply weren't a part of who I was anymore. I had grown and changed, and rather than holding on to these objects of manifestations of my past self, I knew that moving forwards meant letting them go. I had been unwittingly holding myself back from becoming my future self by keeping myself surrounded by these objects chosen by a past, different version of me.

Thinking about my objects in this way was a huge moment. Yes I loved those plastic toadstool ornaments when I was fourteen and obsessed with kawaii culture, but did I want them on display now? No, not really. I imagined my teenage self finding these objects in a charity shop and being delighted by them. I wanted to give someone else that experience. My lukewarm nostalgia paled in comparison, and I donated them.

Who I am now is a product of all those phases I went through. My growth was informed by elements of those times, but what I learned has been kept inside of me, not in those objects.

This shift in my way of thinking went on to affect not only my home, but also my mindset around my identity. I started to feel much more confident in who I really was, underneath the fashion trends and external interests and fads. I was different in my interactions with others too. I had been a people-pleaser for many years, but started to ask myself "what do *I* want?" I started standing up for myself, asking for what I wanted, and allowing myself to truly be myself. I began thinking more deeply about what I wanted my life to be like, and gradually realised that I could actually make those things happen, and all it took to get started was the bravery to believe that I could.

That evening I packed up several bags of clothes and toiletries and early the next morning I dropped them at the women's shelter. I remember feeling a tangible weight lift from my chest as I left, and I think I actually laughed out loud on my drive home, from the realisation that it really was that simple. That I didn't have to worry any more.

Of course, that feeling of elation was interspersed over the following months by moments of frustration, overwhelm, indecision, fear, and sadness. But those moments of freedom outweighed all the others, and gradually the harder feelings became less regular as I learned to truly forgive my past mistakes and focus on my future.

It was a life-changing process, and I am *so very* excited for you that you have chosen this path too!

www.chirp-home.co.uk
Instagram: @chirp_ltd

Onwards to Organised www.chirp-home.co.uk

Before we begin

My approach:

The way I work has always been to encourage my clients to lead the process. While many people experience similar challenges, each person's way of thinking is unique. I find that guiding each client towards making their own disoveries and resolutions is far more empowering and long lasting than using a prescriptive system.

My aim is to equip you to deal with current and future challenges in a way which makes sense in the context of your own circumstances and personality.
I believe in a balance between recognising our limitations, and striving to be the best versions of ourselves. I encourage you to take responsibility for your choices, and I hope that you will feel empowered to trust in your resourcefulness.

Language used:

I use the word "clutter" as a short hand to describe any objects which are not being used for their intended purpose, are stopping a space being used for its intended purpose, or have become burdensome.

The word is in no way meant to be disrespectful to your possessions, only to categorise items not bringing value to your home and life.

While writing this workbook I have tried my best to avoid any kind of judgemental language, and hope that I have succeeded. I take an approach of replacing judgement with curiosity, and encourage my clients to do the same. I find that this invites understanding rather than shame, and puts us in a future-facing midset, where we can freely explore the possibilities that could come from making different choices.

How I wrote this workbook:

This workbook is the amalgamation of tried and tested techniques which I have used with my clients over the last few years.

They come from a combination of professional training, workshops, personal experience, and observing what works well for a variety of different clients.

How to use this workbook

This workbook is for you. This is your time.

I'd like to invite you to please use it however works best for you. It is intended as a spring board for your own journey, rather than a rigid process.

You might like to work through it systematically from beginning to end, or flip through it and dip in here and there. It's totally up to you.

Highlight it, make notes on it, bookmark it, add post-its, make it your own.

Some sections and topics will resonate with you more than others. You if you find yourself thinking "I like the idea of this, but I would do it differently." Please do! I actively encourage you to consider what I have said, evaluate how it applies to you, and adapt it to what makes sense in the context of your own life and home. There are no strict rules here.

A guide to symbols:

When you see this kind of sliding scale, it represents finding a balance or 'sweet spot' between two extremes.

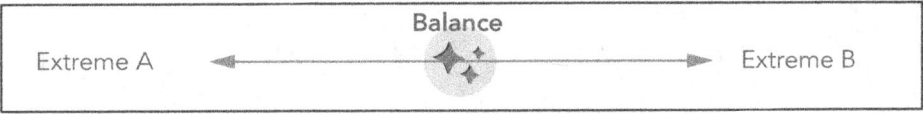

I use the following symbols to show key points.

 Growing point: An opportunity to learn and grow.

 Be kind to yourself: A reminder to use gentle self-talk.

 Reflection point: Something to ponder, discuss or journal about.

 Idea to try: Why not give this a go.

 Mindset shift: Challenge your way of thinking.

Contents

Section 1: Mindset

1. The iceberg
2. Worksheet: How things stand
3. Worksheet: How things stand
4. Worksheet: Letting go
5. Circle of control
6. Circle of control
7. Worksheet: Circle of control
8. Coming up against discomfort
9. Worksheet: Uncomfortable emotions
10. Self Talk
11. Self Talk
12. Worksheet: Self talk
13. Identity
14. Identity
15. Worksheet: My identity
16. Worksheet: What would an XYZ person do?
17. Worksheet: How could I become an XYZ person?
18. Perfectionism
19. Perfectionism
20. Worksheet: Celebration page

Section 2: Planning

21. CHIRP goal setting
22. Worksheet: CHIRP goals
23. Planning ladder
24. Worksheet: Planning ladder
25. Time planning
26. Worksheet: Time planning

27. Weekly and daily planners
28. Worksheet: Weekly planner
29. Worksheet: Daily planner
30. Routine for habit building
31. Routine for habit building
32. Daily routine annotated example
33. Procrastination
34. Procrastination - Overwhelm
35. Procrastination - Underwhelm
36. Worksheet: Procrastination
37. The wiggly line of change
38. Worksheet: The wiggly line of change

Section 3: Action

39. Getting going
40. Push vs pull
41. Zoom in, zoom out
42. Worksheet: Zoom in, zoom out
43. Parting with objects
44. Parting with objects
45. Parting with objects
46. Parting with objects
47. Worksheet: Letting go
48. Quantities
49. The flow of objects
50. Worksheet: The flow of objects
51. Shopping
52. Shopping
53. Shopping: Questions
54. Worksheet: Weighing up a purchase

55. Consumables: Stock control
56. Consumables: Stock control
57. Worksheet: Stock control
58. Gifts
59. Gifts
60. Gifts
61. Worksheet: Clutter free gifting
62. Space planning and storage
63. Space planning and storage
64. Containers

Section 4: Onwards

65. Worksheet: Reflection
66. Worksheet: Reflection
67. Onwards
68. Resources

Section 1

Mindset

The iceberg

When decluttering and organising there are, broadly, two angles to approach from: on the surface or beneath the surface.

The surface is about what we can see happening: working this way is about making changes to our actions and the physical environment, in order to change how we feel inside. **Beneath the surface** is everything going on inside our heads: working this way is about making changes to our way of thinking in order to inform our actions and physical environment.

My approach is to alternate between the two, working from both directions. Switching frequently reduces overwhelm in either area, and can keep you moving forwards. I believe that this holistic approach is the best way to create lasting change.

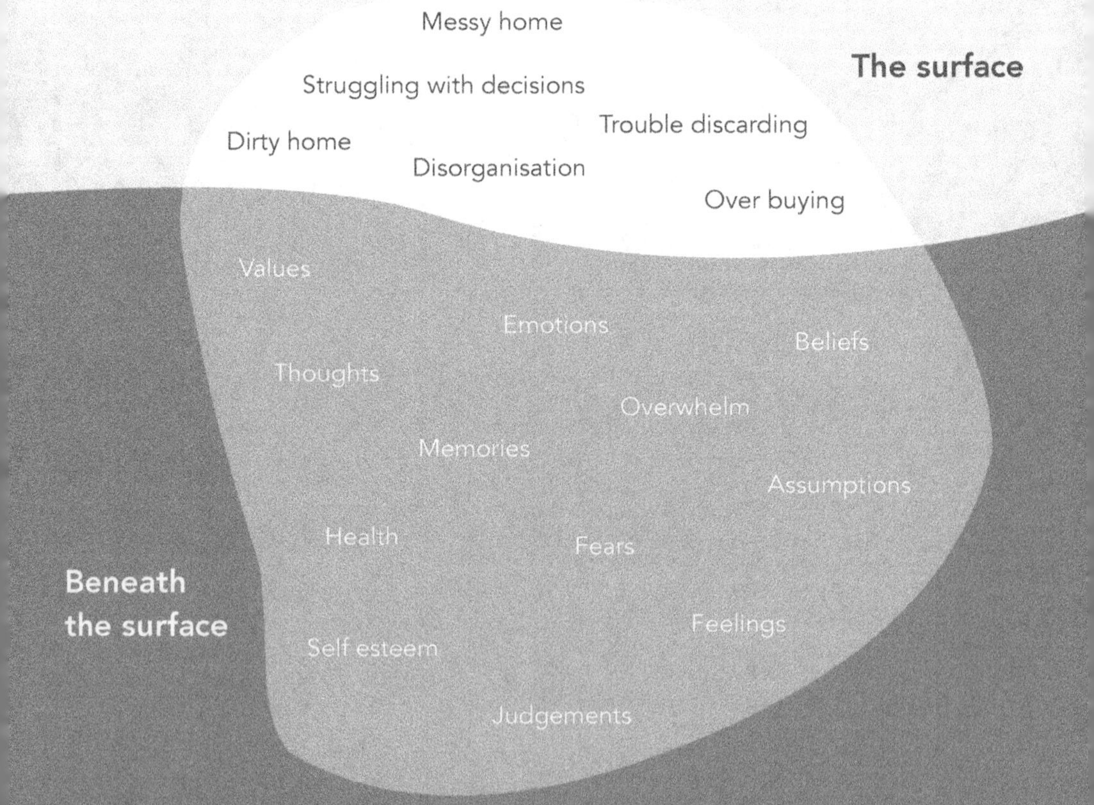

The surface

- Messy home
- Struggling with decisions
- Dirty home
- Trouble discarding
- Disorganisation
- Over buying

Beneath the surface

- Values
- Emotions
- Beliefs
- Thoughts
- Overwhelm
- Memories
- Assumptions
- Health
- Fears
- Feelings
- Self esteem
- Judgements

How things stand

Let's start by acknowledging the current situation. It's not uncommon to put on a brave face for friends and family, and avoid describing the truth of the situation. I'd like to invite you to be as honest as possible. This is just for you, nobody else.

Write as much detail as you would like about the current situation, your physical setting as well as your thoughts and feelings.

What has led you to engage in this process?

Thoughts:

Feelings:

How things stand

Can you identify any obstacles which stand in your way? (These might have made it hard to overcome these challenges in the past.)

Which of these obstacles are external (other people or your environment) and which are internal (your own thoughts and feelings)?

What resources do you have to assist with this process (Help available to you, as well as your own personal strengths and skills)?

Letting go

Decluttering and organising can be very confronting as it brings us face to face with past decisions, and we might feel regret about mistakes we've made.

Throughout this workbook I will be encouraging you to think about the present and the future, rather than the past. Dwelling on the past cannot change it. We are where we are now.

Rather than focussing on past experiences or mistakes, think about how they could inform your future actions.

You might find it helpful to visualise transforming each heavy, negative feeling into a bubble, and letting it drift away. Give yourself permission to let a few things go:

The circle of control

The circle of control is a tool which is helpful for combatting overwhelm and deciding where to spend your energy.

The levels of control or influence can be used to identify the different factors contributing to a situation, and to help you to decide what action can be taken, and where to draw the line under your efforts.

Control
What I do. What I say. My choices. How I direct my thoughts. What I do to improve my mindset.

Influence
The outcome of my actions. My contribution to wider issues. How my day goes. People I interact with.

No control
My past actions. The actions of strangers. Unpredictable circumstances. My genes. The weather.

No control: Everything else
Influence: My surroundings
Control: My own actions

The coloured areas are intentionally smaller at the centre. There is far more outside of our control than inside of it.

By accepting that some things are outside of your control, and letting these things go, you can save wasted time and energy to use in more helpful ways.

By accepting responsibility for your actions and taking ownership of your decisions, you can build your sense of integrity and self esteem.

Circle of control - example

When a scenario is overwhelming or complicated, try using the template on the next page to categorise the different factors.

Control: use these factors to plan your actions.
Influence: factors which you could request or contribute to.
No control: work towards acceptance of these factors.

Here is an example:

Scenario:
My home has fallen into chaos after a period of illness.

Control: what is within my power, what can I do?
Taking action one step at a time.
Committing to the process of change.
Resting, eating well, and doing my exercises to aid my recovery.

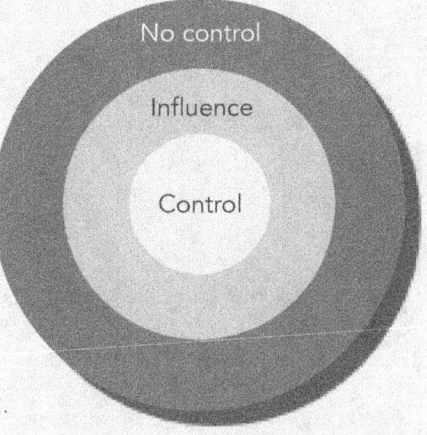

Influence: what can I ask for or contribute to, but not fully control?
Overall progress with tidying up.
My body's recovery.
The kind of help I receive from others.

No control: what is entirely dependent on external factors?
The past few months which led to the current circumstances.
The reactions of other people.
My limitations due to my illness.

Circle of control

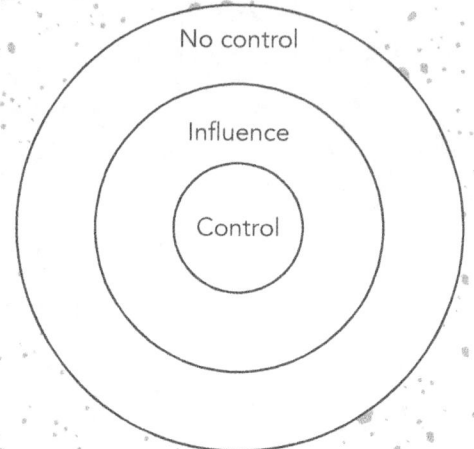

Control: Take action

Influence: Ask/Contribute

No control: Accept

Scenario:

Control: what is within my power, what can I do?

Influence: what can I ask for or contribute to, but not fully control?

No control: what is entirely dependent on external factors?

Coming up against discomfort

Decluttering and organising can be a very confronting process: you are likely to come up against some uncomfortable emotions. For many people this discomfort can seem too much to cope with, and stops us from making progress.

Overwhelm: "There's so much to deal with. I don't know where to start. I'll never get it done."

Shame: "I'm embarrassed that it's got to this point. I don't want anyone to see my home like this."

Regret: "I've wasted money on things I bought and never used. I never gave that gift. I never got into that hobby."

Guilt: "I feel awful about throwing this away. I don't want it to go to landfill. I don't want to offend the person who bought it for me."

Judgement: "I'm a (x) kind of person because of my clutter."

Be kind to yourself:

I hear expressions of these feelings all the time in my work. You are very much not alone.

Remember that just because a thought arises, it doesn't mean it's true or a full picture of the situation. Having these feelings is unpleasant, and often leads people to speak unkindly to themselves. This critical voice is likely to make you feel worse and demotivate you from making progress.

Consider how a kind friend would speak to you about these feelings. Throughout this workbook I will encourage you to use a kind voice when speaking to yourself. You might imagine yourself speaking to a friend, or a friend speaking to you, or invent your own kind character.

Uncomfortable emotions

What qualities does my kind voice have?

The emotion I am having:

What my critical voice is saying:

What would my kind voice say?

The emotion I am having:

What my critical voice is saying:

What would my kind voice say?

The emotion I am having:

What my critical voice is saying:

What would my kind voice say?

Self talk

In addition to responding to uncomfortable emotions, our critical inner voice can pop up at other moments in our lives, often as an immediate response when we make a mistake.

This critical voice might speak inside our head, out loud to ourself, or when speaking about ourself to somebody else.

Its very normal to have these thoughts if you are frustrated by a mistake you've made. However, when you repeat negative statements about yourself you are actually re-inforcing your belief that those statements are true.

Instead:
First take a moment to allow yourself to feel and acknowledge whatever emotions have come up.

Next:
Remember that you don't have super powers. Making mistakes is an inevitable part of being a complicated human navigating the world. A bad decision doesn't make you a bad person.

Moving forwards:
Consider what your intentions were, and what went wrong. What might you learn from this mistake, and how could it inform your future decisions?

Mindset shift:

Berating yourself for making a mistake is unlikely to help you to do better next time. It might actually lower your self esteem, re-inforce the negative traits you are criticising yourself for, and hold you back from learning and growing.

By moving on from our mistakes gently we can gather lessons to help us to do things differently in the future.

Simultaneously acknowledging these two points can seem tricky:

1. We are all fallible creatures. Mistakes are inevitable despite our best efforts.
2. We have the potential to learn, grow and do better.

But accepting you are not perfect while also empowering yourself to believe in your ability to do better can help you to address mistakes in a productive way.

Growing point:
 This way of thinking can empower you to take ownership of your decisions, even if they didn't work out as you had hoped, because you know that you have learnt something and will act differently next time.

| Harsh self-criticism | ← Curiosity, learning, growth → | Unexamined decisions |

Next time you notice yourself using negative self talk use the templates on the next page to reflect on your intentions and needs, and what you might do differently next time.

What I said:
"I bought a pair of shoes I can't walk in because I'm stupid."

My feelings:
Shame and regret.

The intention of my actions:
To feel better after after a tough week.

What went wrong:
My desire to feel special and glamorous outweighed my sense of practicality.

What I could do next time:
Find a way to meet my needs without shopping. Spend an evening with good friends who make me feel special.

Self talk

What I said:

My feelings:

The intention of my actions:

What went wrong:

What I could do next time:

What I said:

My feelings:

The intention of my actions:

What went wrong:

What I could do next time:

What I said:

My feelings:

The intention of my actions:

What went wrong:

What I could do next time:

Identity

The way you view your own identity can affect your mindset, and in turn your actions. This can be both helpful and unhelpful.

If you believe: "I'm a sociable person" you might feel confident going into social situations. You don't worry about whether you'll be able to hold conversations because you know you have things to say and listening skills, and you acklowledge that sometimes conversation just doesn't flow, and that's OK. You let yourself have a fair try.

If, on the other hand, you believe "I'm not a sociable person." You might get nervous before social situations, and panic at the first sign of a lull in conversation. Having the expectation that you won't be able to hold conversation means you might not allow yourself to fully give it a go, because you don't believe the outcome could possibly be positive.

I call this "getting in your own way" and it can become a self-fulfilling prophecy. If we start off believing that the only possible outcome is failure, we are likely to direct ourselves that way, and overlook opportunities for success.

Be kind to yourself:

A harsh and critical inner voice might say something like: "Why am I like this? I always mess things up." Try to counter this with a kind voice. You are trying your best. Each time you try there are opportunities to learn and grow.

Reflection point:

Try to reflect with curiosity rather than judgement. Could you spot any moments when you got in your own way? What beliefs about yourself informed these moments? How could you challenge those beliefs?

The trouble with these beliefs about our identity is that they often feel true to us even without any real world evidence.

They might represent of a past version of ourself, or have no truth to them at all. It takes examination and exploration to discover whether we are really who we think we are.
We might think we are "not an organised person" but we might not be allowing ourselves a fair chance to be.

It can sometimes feel safer to intentionally avoid opportunities for progress or growth. It gives us a sense of security to feel that we know ourselves, and the confirmation that we were right is reassuring, even if it is harmful.

It can feel daunting to aim for more because we open ourselves up to the possibility of failure.

You can't fail if you don't try. But you also can't succeed.

Failures are inevitable on the path of progress, and are not a sign that we were wrong to try. They can teach us valuable lessons and inform future decisions.

Idea to try:

We are so often told to be modest and to downplay our strengths.

Try asking a close friend "what kind of person am I?" you might be pleasantly surprised by their answers.

Mindset shift:

It might seem scary to discover that we aren't who we thought we were. However, it doesn't change our identity, just helps us to gain an accurate understanding of ourself. This is the first step towards growth.

What words would you use to describe yourself?

What words would your friends use to describe you?

What identity traits do you actively lean into?

Do these traits ever cause you problems or get in your way?

What identity traits do you actively avoid or reject?

Could any aspects of of these "negative" traits be helpful to you?

What would a XYZ person do?

What strengths do you personality traits give you?

> You might consider some of your personality traits as weaknesses, but in what way might they be viewed as strengths?

What abilities do these strengths give you?

What kind of person do you aspire to be?

If you were that kind of person, how might your thinking be different?

How might your actions be different?

> Try to use positive statements, rather than negative ones.
> Eg: Instead of "I wouldn't make impulse purchases" try "I would be intentional in my buying habits."

How could I become an XYZ person?

Start with your last answer from the previous page:

What kind of actions would you be taking if you were an XYZ person?

If this was the way you lived your life, how would you think about things?

How would you describe yourself if you were that kind of person?

What are the strengths of being that kind of person?

Can you spot any signs (however small) of any of those strengths in yourself currently? Where do they show up? How could you practise using these strengths more?

It takes bravery to believe in yourself and your potential. It's OK if you find it difficult at first.

Perfectionism

For many people a barrier for getting started is the worry that we won't be able to complete the task perfectly.

This might not show up as a conscious thought. It might look like putting off the task; freezing when we try to start; or feeling like it's not the right moment but not being able to say why.

When we believe that anything other than perfect is a failure, we are trapped by perfectionism.

This "all or nothing" thinking drains our energy and stops us making progress. The task becomes bigger and bigger in our minds, overwhelming us and depleting our resources to tackle it.

Each time we put off a task with no firm plan of when we will tackle it, the task uses our energy without producing any progress. This can become a draining cycle of inaction.

Getting started can be the most challenging part of the process. If you can find a way that works for you to move from inaction to action, keeping going is likely to feel less difficult.

It can be helpful to test out a few ways of getting started:
- Set a limit:
    - Just do 10 minutes, or five minutes, or one minute
    - Do as much as you can while the kettle boils
    - Just do one item from the list.
- Go to the place where the task will happen.
- Do a preparation task (eg: put away dry dishes in preparation for doing the washing-up.)

Chipping away gradually in small chunks will get you into the habit of getting started, quietening perfectionism, and allow you to build up to making more progress when you're ready.

I'd like to invite you to embrace "good enough" as an outcome, and to aim for progress over perfection.

| Not started | Enough | Completed perfectly |

You might find yourself procrastinating as a result of perfectionism. Procrastination is a complex process with multiple causes (more on this in section two) but in the case of perfectionism it can show up as getting side-tracked by easy but unimportant tasks, in order to put off or delay having to start more important but challenging tasks.

You can use these "quick win" tasks as a way to get you started (but I recommend setting a timer to make sure there is time for the main task) or as rewards after you have completed important tasks.

Be kind to yourself:

It takes bravery to challenge perfectionism. You are standing up for yourself against unrealistic expectations. It may never feel easy, but with practice you can get used acknowledging the discomfort and not letting it stand in your way.

Celebrating your progress can give you a sense of achievement and motivation. It can also help to remind yourself of how capable you are, and challenge the negative voice of perfectionism.

Use the next page to note achievements, big or small, that you are proud of.

Celebration page

Mega Win!

Section 2

Planning

CHIRP goal setting

Being clear about your goals is the first step in working to achieve them. If your goal is too vague, or your focus too loose it's easy for goals to slip away.

Try using this acronym to set an intention towards your goal:

C — **Clear** - make sure your goal is well defined. If necessary break it into several smaller goals.

H — **How will you know?** - Decide on what evidence you will be looking out for to recognise you have achieved your goal.

I — **Important** - Why do you want to achieve this goal? What will it mean to you?

R — **Reasonable** - Make sure to set sensible parameters to make sure the goal is attainable.

P — **Period of time** - How long will you give yourself to achieve this goal? Do you have a deadline based on other factors?

Idea to try:

In addition to clarifying your goal in this way, you might find it helpful to create a vision board using inspirational images, quotes and phrases. Focus on the "How will you know" and "Important" sections above. Imagine yourself having achieved the goal. What will it look like? What will it feel like? What will you be doing? You can create vision boards digitally using Pinterest or Canva, or physically with paper and glue, or by writing and drawing in a journal.

CHIRP goal setting

C Clear

H How will you know?

I Important

R Reasonable

P Period of time

Key Words

How will I feel?

Inspiring Quote

Planning ladder

Once you have your goal clearly defined, it can still feel overwhelming to imagine how you might get from where you are now to achieving your goal. Working backwards can help.

Start by writing your goal at the top of the ladder. Next think about what the last step, or finishing touch, would be before you reach that goal. Write this action next to step 7.

Continue working backwards, thinking about what would have needed to have happened already in order to take the action you have just written.
Eventually you will reach the bottom of the ladder. This is your first step.
You can then revisit the CHIRP goal model to set a timescale for each step, and break it down further with it's own ladder if needed.

Example:

Goal: To have my friends stay for the weekend.	Goal
7. Hoover and dust the spare bedroom and put on clean bedsheets.	7
6. Neatly put away the things currently laying on the bed and floor.	6
5. Clear some space in the cupboards by reducing the amount of stuff stored.	5
4. Decide what's to be kept and what can be donated.	4
3. Pull out one box at a time, and find out what's in them.	3
2. Put a date in my diary to set aside to doing this work.	2
1. Make a plan for unwanted items - research local charity shops.	1

Planning ladder

Goal	Goal
7	7
6	6
5	5
4	4
3	3
2	2
1	1

Time planning

It can often feel like we just don't have enough hours in the day to do the things we need to do. There are so many demands on our energy and attention, and balancing those things can be difficult.

I recommend making a written to-do list as a starting point. Having all your tasks set out in front of you rather than holding them in your head will save you mental energy and help you to prioritise.

Non-negotiable - Important and time sensitive:
These are items which must be done at certain times. They might be vital to your health or wellbeing or commitments to others.

Schedule - Important but not time sensitive:
Items which need doing, but which are flexible as to when they get done.

The cherry on the cupcake - Optional and flexible:
Items which are beneficial but not vital. They are important in their own way, but can be easily moved around your schedule.

If your list is very top heavy when putting items into these categories, think about whether you could you ask for some help with certain tasks, or delegate them entirely.

On the other hand, how do you feel and function when you skip self-care and personal enrichment activities? If you get a sense that you function less well when you skip yoga, that task belongs in a different category.

Time planning

1 Non-negotiable - Important and time sensitive

2 Schedule - Important but not time sensitive

3 The cherry on the cupcake - Optional and flexible

Weekly and daily planners

Once you have your list of activities it's time to slot them into your timetable.

You can start with either a weekly planner or a daily planner. There's no right or wrong order, you might even find it helpful to work on both in tandem.

1 Start by filling in the non-negotiables. (This might include work days/hours, appointments, family commitments, hours of sleep etc)

2 Next slot in the tasks which need to be scheduled. (These might be errands, house work, life admin etc)

3 Finally see what time you can block out to use for cherry on the cupcake activities.

Remember to allow enough time for any preparation, journey time, and tidying up time for each activity.

When unexpected events arise during your day, refer back to the three categories, and try asking yourself these questions:
- Does it need to be dealt with immediately?
- Could it be scheduled for later in the day/week?
- Could you ask somebody else to help?
- Does it need to be done at all? It's OK to say no!

Be kind to yourself:

 Creating a planner is all about setting out an ideal version of how you would like your day to go. But don't worry if things don't go to plan. On the following pages we'll talk more about adjusting routines through trial and error.

Weekly planner

am ⟶ pm

Monday

Tuesday

Wednesday

Thursday

Friday

Saturday

Sunday

Daily planner

Type of routine:

Time	Activity

Routine for habit building

Turning a daily plan into a routine means that you save energy planning and making decisions. Creating a realistic plan is key to getting a routine to stick.

Give yourself a chance to test out your daily and weekly plans from the previous pages, and then annotate them to show how things actually happened.
Try to be as accurate and truthful as possible.

Example:

Desired Routine:

07:30 - Get up and do some stretches
07:45 - Have a shower
08:05 - Have breakfast
08:20 - Prepare to leave the house
08:25 - Leave the house
08:55 - Arrive at work

What happened:

07:30 - First alarm
07:45 - Second alarm
08:00 - Get up
08:05 - Drink coffee and scroll social media
08:20 - Have a shower
08:35 - Leave the house
09:05 - Arrive at work

Reflection point:

If you find that your reality is very different from your desired routine, try asking yourself:
- Am I allowing myself enough time for each activity?
- Am I trying to fit too much in?
- Am I trying to change too much at once?
- Am I feeling motivated to make these changes? Can I see the value in what these changes will bring me? What's stopping me?

After a period of repetition, doing the same activities one after another creates a series of events. One activity leads to the next and you move from one to another without having to consciously think about it.

This can be unhelpful when you fall into repeated patterns which are getting in the way of your progress (for example always scrolling on your phone as soon as you wake up) but you can use this to your advantage if you adapt your series of events to include helpful habits (for example, always putting your plate straight into the dishwasher when you finish eating.)

Growing point:

If you are aiming to build a new daily habit from scratch, consider starting with a very short period of time and building on it.
For example: rather than "tidy the house for an hour" try "tidy the house for five minutes" Once you are consistently sticking to doing it regularly, then add more time.

Be kind to yourself:

It can take some time to get into the groove of a routine. It can feel like a lot of effort at first while you are adapting.
Don't expect to get it right first time. It's absolutely a process of trial and error, experimenting with different timings, and adapting to life's changes over time.

We all have difficult times in our lives, and during these times it's common for our routines to go out the window somewhat.
If this happens, pare back to your non-negotiables, and gradually add items back in as you feel ready.

Daily planner (annotated example)

Type of routine: Weekday Evenings

Time	Activity
18:00	Get in from work — *Put a box file in the hallway*
	Sort post into piles for filing and recycling
	Change into comfy clothes — *Some days I didn't bother, that's OK*
18:20	Put on some music and cook dinner
19:00	Eat dinner — *I didn't do this, try some yoga instead, and do it before dinner*
19:30	Go for a 15 minute walk
19:45	Do something creative or social — *Need to add time for life admin*
22:00	Put phone on 'do not disturb'
	Get ready for bed: skincare routine
	Read book — *I kept going back to scrolling social media. I need to find my motivation.*
23:00	Lights out

Procrastination

Many people associate procrastination with laziness - I do not agree!
In my experience, procrastination can be the product of several different challenges. Working out where your procrastination is coming from is the first step in challenging it.

Everyone is different, but I find that procrastination can often fit into two styles: **overwhelm** and **underwhelm**. One person might also experience both depending on the circumstances.

Overwhelm - too much pressure

- Fear of failure (re-visit the page on perfectionism for a refresher on this).
- Trouble seeing steps required to complete a task.
- Feeling frozen under pressure from external judgement.

The feeling of overwhelm can lead to avoiding the task, which may increase the size of the task, which builds more overwhelm, and this becomes a draining cycle. The discomfort suffered anticipating the task becomes linked to the task, and can create a sense of dread.

Underwhelm - not enough pressure

- No urgency or sense of purpose.
- Trouble priotising.
- Avoiding boring and repetitive tasks.

Underwhelm can show up as de-prioritising almost everything, saying that you can do it later, or getting distracted by more exciting options. This can lead to a cycle of putting things off until the last minute and then rushing to try to get everything done.

Tips for overwhelm

If it takes less than 5 minutes do it now.
If it takes less than 30 minutes do it today.
If it takes more time, put it in your schedule.

Confide in a trusted friend who will cheer you on.

Growing point:

If you feel frozen under the pressure of other people's expectations, try defining your own. Deciding what's important to you and what you really want, regardless of what is expected of you, can be a liberating exercise,

Idea to try:

Get started on a task before the spiral of nervous anticipation gets too far. If your usual approach is to think through tasks carefully before starting, you may find it helpful to practise diving in with as little thought and planning as possible.

Mindset shift:

Gently question your excuses. Are you inflating the challenges of the task in order to stop yourself from getting started? Do your reasons reflect reality?

Speak kindly to yourself, and consider how you might empower yourself to overcome or work around these obstacles.

Tips for underwhelm

Never put a task off for "later" without scheduling in when "later" will be.

Make a task more appealing by combining it with something you find enjoyable. Eg: putting on some music while washing up.

Reflection point:

If you find that you are de-prioritising important tasks, try reflecting on what completing these tasks will mean for you. Putting them in the context of your values, goals, or ability to engage in more enjoyable experiences can help to add purpose to unappealing tasks.

Idea to try:

If you find that you work better under pressure :

- Set a timer and commit to finishing a task in that time. (Or during the ad break, or while the kettle boils).
- Use rewards or penalties to help you to commit to tasks.

If you find accountability helpful:

- Ask a friend to come over or phone at an agreed time to make sure you have done the task.
- Ask them to sit with you (either in person or over the phone) while you get it done.

Procrastination

An instance when I have noticed myself procrastinating:

What thoughts am I having while I'm procrastinating?

Does this feel like overwhelm or underwhelm?

Which ideas from the previous pages resonate with me?

Try out some of the methods and record your experience:

The wiggly line of change

Making changes to behaviour and forming habits are not linear processes.
It would be unusual to cut off unhelpful behaviour, or embed a new habit into your life without having some slip-ups along the way.
Putting this expectation on yourself can be unhelpful, as feeling that you have "failed" can be a demotivator.

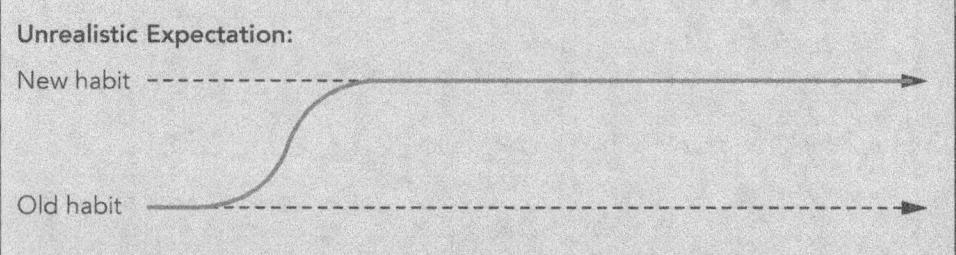

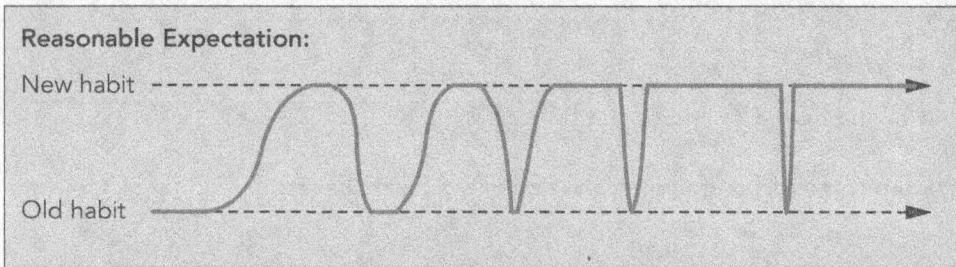

Growing Point:

It's very normal to have "blips" along the way. Each time this happens try to reflect on what happened. What could you learn from the situation to help you next time?

Reset and pick up where you left off. Don't discount the steps you have taken forwards, even when you take a few steps back.

Use the worksheet on the next page to learn from your next blip.

The wiggly line of change

New behaviour:

Old behaviour:

What might have contributed to this "blip"?

What can I learn from this experience? What might I do differently next time?

A reminder of the progress I have already made:

My action plan for resetting and picking up where I left off:

Section 3

Action

getting going

Once you are ready to get started, it can be helpful to get into the right mindset by setting your intentions. You might do this in the moment, or the day before.

Setting intentions is all about consciously committing to what you plan to do.

Write it down:
Make a task list, write your intentions as a letter to yourself, or outline your plans in a journal.

Journalling can be helpful as you can then write your reflections later.

Tell a friend:
Speak to a trusted friend about your plans and enjoy their encouragement.

Take care:
Make sure you have had enough sleep, are warm/cool enough, have eaten and are hydrated.

Set the scene:
Choose an outfit that you will wear to do your work. Laying it out the night before can help to follow up on your intention.

Make a playlist of music that will make you feel good, or put on a motivational podcast.

Meditation:
It can be really powerful to visualise yourself carrying out your plan and seeing the results.

Walking it through in your mind can prepare you to get started.

Be careful not to let your preparations get in the way of actually getting started.
- Don't use up all your time creating the perfect playlist.
- Don't let "less than perfect conditions" become a barrier.
- Re-visit the circle of control: do what you can and accept what you can't.

Push vs pull

When decluttering it's really common to find it difficult to let go of objects. I find that our reasons for keeping things generally fit into two categories: Push and Pull.

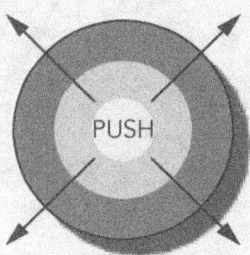

Push:
"I can't let that go." "I can't deal with that right now." "I feel bad when I think about that."

Guilt. Shame. Fear.

Perhaps it was an unwanted gift, belonged to a loved one, cost a lot of money, or never got used.

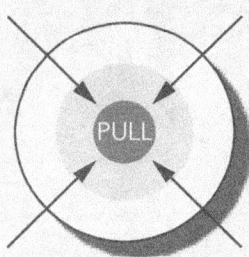

Pull:
"I love this." "This is useful to me." "I feel good when I think about this."

Enjoyment. Passion. Utility.

An object which serves a purpose, something we genuinely want in our lives..

Idea to try:

Sometimes pushes can present themselves as pulls. It can help to speak or write about the object. Try asking yourself:
- Would I spend money to acquire this object today?
- If nobody else's opinion mattered would I still want it?
- If I had permission to let it go would I still want it?
- What is the function of this object? Will I realistically fulfil that function?

Zoom in, zoom out

Zoom in: If you are overwhelmed by the scale of your task, try focussing in on the individual parts which make up the whole.

For example: When decluttering your kitchen start with one drawer at a time, or one type of object at a time. Once you have zoomed in, look for other categories and zoom again. Do this as many times as you need to until you are left with a single decision to make.

Your process could look something like:
Declutter the kitchen > start inside the cupboards > start with the drawers > start with the top drawer > declutter the cooking utensils > reduce the amount of spatulas > donate this spatula.

> If you are feeling overwhelmed it can be helpful to do one of these two completely opposite things. Try alternating between the two if you find yourself getting stuck.

Zoom out: If you are getting bogged down in the details of individual objects, try looking at your decisions in the context of your life as a whole.

For example: When deciding whether you want to keep or discard an item think about it in the context of its category, what that category means to you, and how it measures up against other areas of your life.

Your process could look something like:
I don't know what to do about this DVD < I enjoyed it at the cinema but haven't watched it in years < within my DVDs collection this is not one of my favourites < my goal is to make space on these shelves for board games < achieving my goal more important than this DVD.

Zoom in, zoom out

Zoom in

What is the over-all area or task?

What are the components of this area or task?

Pick one of these components. Break this down further into specifics.

Pick one of these specifics. What is your course of action for this thing individually?

What are you focussed on?

What category is this part of?

Where does this category sit compared to others?

How do you view this object in the wider context of your life?

Zoom out

Parting with objects

Even if you know that an object does not serve a purpose in your life any more, you might still find it hard part with it.
It's OK to feel this way, it's not uncommon, and it's not silly.

Choose what to keep

Rather than choosing what you are getting rid of, instead choose what you will keep.

Selecting and celebrating key objects for their usefulness or enjoyability can help you to build a curated selection of "keepers". This then becomes the criteria by which to compare other objects being considered.

Allowing space to let these key objects shine will help you to enjoy them, rather than seeing them buried in items which are less valuable to you.

What are you gaining?

Consider the value what you will gain each time you let go of an object.

It could be visual space, mental peace, or activities you could then use the space for.

You could aim to have nothing to trip over on the bedroom floor, or create enough space to do a jigsaw, or make it easier for yourself to clean the worktops.

It can be helpful to consider what gaining that space would mean to you, and re-frame the process in terms of moving towards that goal.

Mindset shift:

Try re-framing the process as giving to yourself, rather than taking away. How will you benefit? What discomfort will you alleviate? How might your life change for the better? Who else might also benefit?

Waste and sustainability

Many people find themselves getting stuck with items which are not in a condition to be donated, and cannot be recycled.

> Common concerns which can come up:
> - I'm contributing to landfill by throwing this away.
> - I'm being wasteful.
> - What if it can be recycled, but I don't know about it?
> - I don't accept that this cannot be recycled. It should be.

For these kind of concerns I would recommend revisiting the the circle of control.

> - What is possible within the current recycling infrastructure?
> - What are my options given my finances, time, and location.
> - What can I do, and what just isn't possible for me.
> - What decisions can I make going forwards?
> - What could I work towards forgiving myself for?

As much as it would be fantastic if we could all live zero-waste lifestyles, the truth of the matter is that for many of us it isn't currently a realistic option.

Until the default and cheapest option is the most sustainable one, many of us are tied to less sustainable options.

I'd like to invite you to choose the areas where you can make a difference, and allow yourself forgiveness for those that you can't. I suggest setting boundaries around the amount of time and energy you will dedicate to researching recycling schemes or sustainable options.

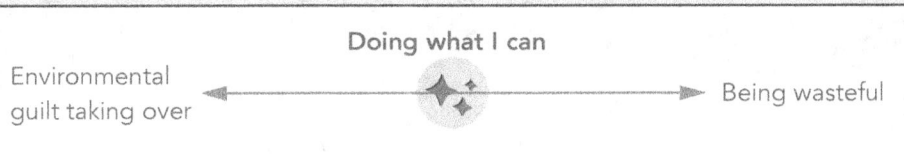

Holding zone

If you are really struggling with making a decision about an object, try setting a reminder to revisit the decision. Create a "holding zone" for these tricky objects. It's important to set a limit on the quantity of these items (perhaps one bag or box) and to commit to coming back to it tomorrow or in a week's time.

Sometimes a bit of unconscious processing time away from decision making can clarify things and make the decision easier.

Skim for quick wins

A less mentally taxing method of surface decluttering is to walk around your home with a box or bag, picking out anything which is a "definite no" and spending no more than a few seconds on each area.

Helping others

Do you have something which could be a comfort to somebody in need?

Could somebody benefit from it at a food bank or shelter?

Could giving it to a charity shop help them to raise money for a cause you care about?

Can you imagine somebody else really loving and enjoying this object?

Could it be a treat for somebody who wouldn't be able to afford to buy this item new?

Could the object serve its purpose better in somebody else's home?

Reflection point:

Sometimes you might know deep down that you don't want to keep something, but you don't feel ready to discard it. Try reflecting on your thoughts about the object: What's stopping you from making the decision? How could you address this before tackling the object itself?

Inherited objects

It can feel particularly difficult to part with objects which belonged to, or remind us of a friend or family member who is no longer with us.

Remember that the person is not contained within the object. Your decision about the object is not a reflection of your respect for their memory.

Do you enjoy re-visiting the memories? Could you evoke those memories in a different way? For example telling stories and speaking to friends who knew the person.

If you don't enjoy re-visting the memories, could you give yourself permission to have freedom from the reminders?

Parting doesn't mean losing

The memories of a person or time which you associate with an object don't exist inside the object. They exist inside you.

By parting with the object you are not removing those memories from yourself.

You will still keep the most important part of those memories, which is your experience of them.

A note about giving objects to friends and family:

It can be tempting to pass on your unwanted items to friends and family, as a way of making sure that they will still be useful to somebody.

There are a few reasons why this can be problematic:
- You may still feel responsibility for the object. If you are giving an object away, you must accept that the recipient has the right to choose what they do with it after it enters their home.
- Make sure to give your friends and family an opportunity to say no. Many people feel obliged to accept items, and perhaps they are also struggling with their own decluttering journey. Be careful not to pass on the burden of decision to them.

Letting go

Use this page to note down helpful and empowering thoughts you have when making decisions about letting objects go.
Come back here as a reminder if you get stuck in the future.

Quantities

I am often asked "What's the right amount?" or "How many is too many?" And the answer is, unfortunately, not that simple!

The right amount for YOU is based on multiple factors:
- How much space do you have available overall?
- How much of that space are you willing to dedicate to that particular kind of item?
- Are your storage systems working well?
- What impact do these items have on your life? Is it positive or negative? Enjoyable or burdensome?

Person A:
"Owning 500 books is fine for me. I have the space to display and access them, I enjoy looking at them, I often re-read them, reading is my favourite hobby."

Person B:
"50 books is too many for me. I don't have the shelf space, I mostly read on my kindle, and I'd like more space for house plants."

It can be tricky to clearly see the total quantity of items you own if they are scattered around the house.

Gathering together "like with like" is a good place to start. This will give you a clear picture of the total volume of your collection.

If this isn't practical for you, try taking photos or making a list.

Consider how long it would take to use the quantity of items you have.
If you have 100 greetings cards, and you send 20 a year, that would take you five years to send them all.

The more of any item you own, the more likely you are to forget about specific items in your collection, and therefore not get round to using or enjoying them. There is a sweet spot between ample choice, and too many to keep track of.

The flow of objects

When you're putting lots of energy into decluttering it's important to also consider objects coming into your home. It can be disheartening to feel that objects are accumulating faster than they are leaving.

Many people find it helpful to implement a "one in, one out" rule, meaning that you must declutter a comparable item if you want to buy something new.

This system can work well as maintenance if are happy overall with the amount of "stuff" you own.

However, if you are still in the process of reducing down, this method isn't quite right. You could change the ratio to "one in, four out" or "one item in, per bag of donations out" or you might try an entirely different method such as abstaining from buying anything in a parcicular category (such as clothes) during your decluttering journey.

Keep an eye on subscription services. Make sure to check in regularly whether the quantity coming in matches your rate of consumption. If you are getting swamped, adjust, pause, or cancel your subscription.

I always encourage buying items which can be used for multiple occasions, but life sometimes requires exceptions.
If you plan to buy something for a particular occasion, try to be honest with yourself; if you won't use it again make sure to sell it or give it away promptly.
Keeping it in the cupboard won't change the fact that you have already spent money on it.

For items which regularly enter your home, it can be helpful to have a strategy to keep on top of accumulation.

For example, magazines: Consider how often you re-visit previous issues. You may have really enjoyed an article, but consider whether you will realistically set aside time in the future to go through your collection to read it.
If you needed that information in the future could you perhaps find it online?

The flow of objects

What do I currently have too much of?

What would feel like the "right amount" of these items to me? (Quantity, volume etc)

What is my plan for removing unwanted items from my home? Where can I dispose of, recycle, donate, or sell?

My strategy for keeping on top of accumulation in the future:

Why is this important to me? How will I remind myself of this?

Shopping

We are constantly being bombarded with messages to buy more stuff. Advertising messages tell us that we will be happier, healthier, and more popular when we purchase the newest trending item. It's little surprise that many people struggle with over-buying and impulse purchases.

Below are some suggestions and points to consider when shopping:

Growing point:

If you know that you **struggle to discard items**, it's important to think about your shopping strategy.

By reducing the amount of objects coming into your home, you will reduce the discomfort of decisions to be made later down the line.

You might also like to **consider buying second hand** rather than new. This gets you involved in the flow of second hand objects. Why not take a bag of donations with you when you next go to a charity shop?

Mindset shift:

When deciding whether to buy something, you may find it helpful to weigh up the benefits of owning the item versus the burden.

All possessions are at least partially a burden to us. We need to find space to store them, keep them clean and functional, and eventually find a way to dispose of them. **An item is worth owning if its contribution to your life outweighs its burden.**

Mindset shift:

Try to critically consider what you are **actually** buying versus what the product is trying to sell you. Advertising campaigns are designed to try to sell you a whole lifestyle, which is not, in fact, what you would receive when you make your purchase. A huge amount of money and expertise is put into advertising, and it is unsurprising that we get drawn in.

Reflection point:

Consider how often you use a particular kind of item to gauge whether a new one will contribute meaningfully to your life, or become clutter. For example: if you have 15 formal dresses, but only go to formal events two or three times a year, it will take you five years to wear them all. In the meantime they will take up valuable space in your wardrobe.

Be kind to yourself:

If you have bought something which you later come to regret I would like to invite you to forgive yourself. Speak to yourself with a kind voice. What would you do differently next time?

You may like to consider donating your unwanted item so that it can be used by somebody else.

If it cannot be donated, can it be recycled? If it can't be recycled, try gently giving yourself permission to throw it away. You are doing your best; you don't need to carry the burden of keeping it to avoid landfill.

Shopping: Questions

Here are a few questions to help you to make your decision when considering a purchase:

- Where will I keep it? Do I have space?

- How often will I use it? Could I borrow or rent it instead?

- Will it serve multiple functions?

- How long will it last? Will it quickly become clutter or rubbish?

- How will I dispose of it when I have finished with it?

- Do I already have something that will serve the same purpose? Do I need multiples?

- Does it work with other items I already have? Would it require more purchasing to make it useable?

- Is it replacing something that's worn out? If so make sure to let the old item go.

Idea to try:

When you want to buy something, take a moment to consider whether you actually want the item, or if you are seeking the thrill of making a purchase.

Pause to take a breath. You might find it helpful to take a photo or bookmark the page, and if you still want it the next day or week, then go back and get it.

Weighing up a purchase

What is the item?

Why do I want it?

Would I still want it if it was full price? Will I still want it in a week's time if I don't buy it now?

What benefit would it bring me?

Will this item bring me this benefit on its own, or does it depend on other factors?

Are these other factors present, achievable, or realistic?

Where will I keep it? Do I have space?

How often will I use it? Will I still be using it in a year's time? Are there options to borrow or rent it instead?

How will I dispose of it when I no longer need it? Can it be fixed if it breaks?

Consumables: Stock control

There are different factors to consider when purchasing items which will be used up, compared to items which will be kept. **Consumables** can refer to foods & drinks, toiletries, cleaning supplies, materials for hobbies etc.

It can be appealing to buy in bulk to get better value for money or take advantage of special offers. Take care, however, to consider whether that saving is enough to outweigh the burden of having to store and organise extra items.

When purchasing consumables consider:
- how long it takes to use
- how much space it takes up.

Type A - Used up quickly - Small	Type B - Used up quickly - Bulky
Type C - Lasts a long time - Small	Type D - Lasts a long time - Bulky

Take care: most items on multi-buy special offer will be Type C & D - this is to raise sales by encouraging you to buy more than you really need.

It might make sense to take advantage of offers on "Type A" which you use lots of on a frequent basis, and "Type B" if you have the space.

Think carefully about buying multiples of "Type C" as they will sit in your cupboard for months or even years. Avoid buying multiples of "Type D".

It's also worth considering how important an item is to you, and whether it takes priority over other items in your available storage space.

As I mentioned on the Quantities sheet, There is no "right" amount of any particular item to have. It will depend on your specific circumstances.
You may find it helpful to create your own set rules when buying consumables.

Eg: Tins of tomatoes.
Quantity used: Maximum of two tins per week.
Packet size: six tins.
Buy: Add to shopping list when three tins remain.

Eg: Hand soap
Quantity used: one bar per month.
Packet size: two bars.
Buy: Add to shopping list when last spare bar is started.

Eg: Sellotape
Quantity used: one roll every six months.
Packet size: one roll.
Buy: Two rolls before Christmas.

Keeping a shopping list on an easily accessible note pad or on your phone is a great way of keeping your stock levels under control. Get into the habit of writing items on the list when you notice you need them, and strictly stick to the list when you go shopping.

It can be tempting to stock up with much more than we need. But how likely is it that you won't be able to get hold of this item when you next need it? Is that possible inconvenience worse than the certain inconvenience of unmanageable cupboards?

If you are buying items outside of everyday consumables (eg: if you are making a trip to a specialist shop) assess exactly how much space you have available to store these items before you go.

If you are buying something because it's on special offer, ask yourself: Would I want this if it was full price? Is it about the product or the thrill of getting a good deal? What are the consequences of that?

If you are buying something which is reduced because of being close to the use-by date, make sure that you can actually use it before it goes out of date. If you can only use half of it before it goes off, even if you only paid half price, you are not getting a good deal.

Stock control

Item	How long it lasts	Stock level	When to next buy

Overstock alert!
(don't buy this for a while)

Gifts

Gift giving is a significant social expectation around events like birthdays or other celebrations.

For some of us it's part of how we show our affection for one another.
For many of us it feels like a lot of pressure, and causes discomfort.
Here are some tips for how to reduce the potential clutter of gift giving.

When giving a gift, try to think past the feelings in the moment of the gift giving. Consider the future of the object in that person's life.

Consider giving and asking for experience gifts. Spending time with your friend or family member will create wonderful memories without the clutter. It's also a way to show them that you enjoy their company.

If you have received a gift that you don't want, it can feel like you have an obligation to keep it. Might you be able to give yourself permission to let it go? Would you want a good friend to feel uncomfortable with an unwanted gift, or would you want them to let it go?

To reduce unwanted gifts consider making a wish list for gifts, and encourage your friends and family to do the same.
You can be as specific or vague as you prefer.

Financial pressures can make gift giving very stressful. Do you have some friends with whom you could mutually agree not to buy gifts?

When buying somebody a gift, think about what you are trying to say to them via the gift. Could you say it in a way that doesn't involve the exchange of an object?

In friendship groups or families consider setting up a "secret santa" where each member only buys and receives one gift within the group.

For some alternatives to traditional gift giving consider the following themes:

Time together:

The activity itself isn't really important, it's more about spending uninterrupted time in each other's company.

A passive activity like walking or having coffee can be less distracting and allow you to be fully present. Put down your phone, turn off the TV and give your friend your full attention.

Connection:

Building the depth of your friendship.
This could be about taking the time to listen, and sharing honestly, telling your friend what you value about them as a person and your friendship.
For groups it could be as simple as getting everyone in the same room together (or on the same video call) or more structured activities.

Exploration:

This is about having new experiences together.
It could be a big adventure like a holiday or a new sport, or a small one like trying a new craft or going to the cinema.

Learning and exploring together can be a great bonding experience and create wonderful memories that you can both enjoy.

Helping out:

This is about providing something really helpful which will ease the burden of your friend's workload and give them more time to do the things they enjoy.

This could be helping out yourself or providing money or vouchers for services.

Some examples of clutter-free gifts.

Time together:

- Going out for a meal
- A spa day
- Going hiking
- Watching a film you both enjoy
- Visiting a friend who lives far away
- Baking or cooking together
- Playing board games
- Crafting together
- Working on a DIY project

Connection:

- Writing letters
- Looking through photos of memorable times
- Visiting a place which is significant to your friendship
- Group holiday
- Group potluck meal
- Group games
- Starting a book or film club
- Having a photoshoot

Exploration:

- Going on holiday
- Taking a class or workshop together
- Going to see a gig or theatre
- Going to the cinema
- Going to a gallery or museum
- Going to a sports match
- Trying a new sport
- Volunteering together

Helping out:

- Babysitting
- Cooking meals
- Recipe box subscription
- Paying for a cleaner, gardener or handyman
- Paying for a class or course
- Vouchers for everyday necessities
- Paying for a subscription to Netflix/Audible/Spotify etc
- Contribute to their holiday fund

Clutter-free gifting

Here are some prompts to help you to explain clutter-free gifting to friends and family.

This year I'm taking part in the Chirp Clutter-Free Gifting Challenge! This is all about reducing the amount of "stuff" given and received during celebrations, and bringing the focus back to connecting with the people who are important to us.

I'd love to try one of the following instead:

Spending time together:

....

....

Feeling connected:

....

....

Exploring a new experience:

....

....

Helping out:

....

....

Something else:

....

....

Space planning and storage

Keeping things tidy is much simpler when your space works *for* you, not *against* you. When choosing where and how things are to be stored, I like to consider "friction points" in the process.

These are anything which gets in the way of you putting something away. Eg: Having to un-stack several boxes to get to the one you need, not having space to store something, or needing a step ladder to reach a high cupboard.

It only takes a very small amount of friction to de-motivate you from putting things away, and the higher the friction the more likely you are to put it off.

Try to create as short a journey as possible between storing and using an item. Either bring the storage to the activity, or bring the activity to the storage. This might mean maximising storage in high-use areas, or maximising functionality in spaces with storage available.

For example:
Approach A: You tend to craft at the table in the sitting room - make space for all your craft supplies in the sitting room.
Approach B: You have lots of empty storage space in your spare room - create a crafting area here.

Ease friction points:

If your clean laundry always ends up sitting around for days because you dislike folding, it's OK to accept this and adapt your system. Try using drawers or baskets which you can easily pile your clothes into. Be kind to yourself and remove the expectation that you have to do things in a certain way.

Consider your limitations:

If you cannot bend to reach a low cupboard, or cannot lift a heavy box, or don't like going into the shed for fear of spiders, avoid using these areas to store items you need access to on a regular basis. (You may also like to consider whether an item which is inaccessible to you is worth keeping.)

It might seem efficient to fill your cupboards to maximum capacity, but if you have to take other things out in order to access the item you need, it adds friction and requires more effort.

Your storage systems should help you out, and make it easy for you to access what you need, rather than forcing you to complete complicated rearranging puzzles each time you need something.

These small moments of effort add up over time and, especially if you are already overwhelmed or frustrated, can drain your energy.

Leaving enough space to see everything in a cupboard or drawer at a glance means that the effort required to find what you're looking for is minimized.

- Group duplicates of the same item together (eg: tins of beans)
- Avoid stacking anything which isn't a duplicate. It creates extra effort if you need to access something half way down the pile. (eg: folded clothes, games)
- Stand flat objects up on their edge so that they can be seen clearly and accessed easily (eg: folded clothes, baking trays)
- Keep drawers to one layer, so that nothing is hidden underneath. Avoid using deep drawers for small objects. (eg: batteries, string)
- Use containers to keep small items together (eg: rubber bands, hair clips)

- Give objects a home.
- Store objects close to where you use them.
- Make objects easy to access.
- Make your system work for you, not the other way around.

Containers

It can be very tempting to rush ahead and buy lots of pretty containers before doing anything else. This understandable when storage solutions are sold to us as the answer to our disorganisation, but the truth is that without a good system in place, these containers will only become clutter themselves.

I recommend establishing your organisational systems well in advance of purchasing any storage solutions.

If and when you do want to buy containers consider the following:
- Measure and plan carefully - take a list of dimensions and quantities with you when you go shopping.
- Square containers make more efficient use of space than circular ones.
- If you are buying a container to decant a product into, make sure it is larger than the full size of a packet so that you aren't left with "dregs" in the original packaging.
- See-through containers allow you to see what's inside immediately without the need for labels.
- Be wary of extremely specific storage solutions, and products which make things fiddlier rather than easier.

You don't have to buy special containers. Re-using what you have can work very well - jam jars, yogurt pots, margarine tubs or cereal boxes.
(Remember that these items come into your home on a regular basis, so no need to collect them - you will always be able to get your hands on one if you need it. You can even ask a friend or neighbour.)

Section 4
Onwards

Reflection

Chirp

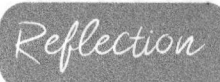

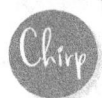

Now that you have reached the end of this workbook, let's take a moment to re-visit your initial answers at the start of the workbook, and reflect on your journey so far.

What would you like to say to the past version of yourself who began this journey?

What changes have you noticed in your thoughts and feelings?

What changes have you noticed in your actions?

What other changes have you noticed?

Reflection

Chirp

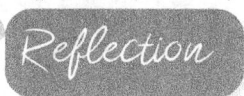

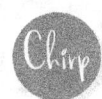

Have your thoughts about your obstacles changed?

Have you identified any other resources which are helpful to you?

What are some positive things you have learned about yourself?

What are some important realisations or lessons you have learned from this process?

What will your next steps be?

Onwards

The end of this workbook is just the start of your journey.

Use the tools and worksheets throughout this book, adapt them as you see fit, repeat your reflections from the previous page, and move onwards to organised.

Here are a few reminders to send you on your way:

Be kind to yourself:

This workbook exists because the kinds of challenges you are facing are common. It might seem like everyone else is getting by with no trouble, but that simply isn't the case. You are not a failure, and you are certainly not alone.

Growing point:

Changes to habits don't happen over-night; they take time and repetition. Try out lots of different approaches, reflect on your progress, get curious about your slip ups, and keep persevering. Even if things slip, you will have the benefit of experience on your side, and won't be starting from scratch.

Mindset shift:

Striving to do better can help us to achieve our goals, but don't let it turn into guilt. Cultivate acceptance of yourself as you are right now. "I have potential to grow, but I am also enough as I am."

Resources

Organisations:

Association of Professional Declutterers and Organisers (APDO)
(Professional organisers operating at home and online around the UK)
www.apdo.co.uk

Hoarding Disorders UK
(Expert advice and practical support for people affected by hoarding)
www.hoardingdisordersuk.org

Recycle Now
(A database of recycling options for different objects and materials)
www.recyclenow.com

Charity Retail Association
(Donation information and database of charity shops in the UK)
www.charityretail.org.uk/find-a-charity-shop

British Association for Counselling and Psychotherapy
(Information about counselling and database of registered practitioners)
www.bacp.co.uk

Books:

Stuff: Compulsive Hoarding and the Meaning of Things - Randy Frost and Gail Steketee

Understanding Hoarding: Reclaim your Space and your Life - Jo Cooke

Atomic Habits - James Clear

How to keep house while drowning - KC Davis

If you found this workbook helpful,
I'd love to hear from you!

You can email me at hello@chirp-home.co.uk or tag me in your experience and progress on Instagram @chirp_ltd

Extra copies of worksheets

Letting go

Decluttering and organising can be very confronting as it brings us face to face with past decisions, and we might feel regret about mistakes we've made.

Throughout this workbook I will be encouraging you to think about the present and the future, rather than the past. Dwelling on the past cannot change it. We are where we are now.

Rather than focussing on past experiences or mistakes, think about how they could inform your future actions.

You might find it helpful to visualise transforming each heavy, negative feeling into a bubble, and letting it drift away. Give yourself permission to let a few things go:

Circle of control

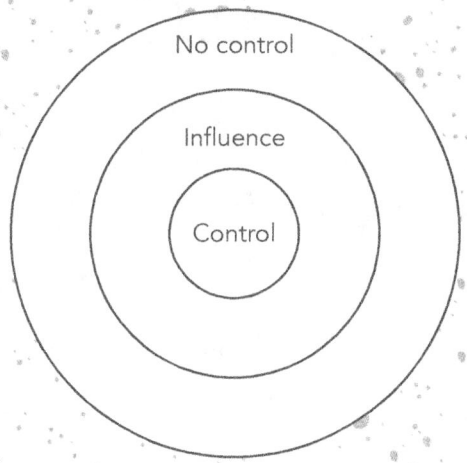

Control: Take action

Influence: Ask/Contribute

No control: Accept

Scenario:

Control: what is within my power, what can I do?

Influence: what can I ask for or contribute to, but not fully control?

No control: what is entirely dependent on external factors?

Uncomfortable emotions

What qualities does my kind voice have?

The emotion I am having:

What my critical voice is saying:

What would my kind voice say?

The emotion I am having:

What my critical voice is saying:

What would my kind voice say?

The emotion I am having:

What my critical voice is saying:

What would my kind voice say?

Self talk

What I said:

My feelings:

The intention of my actions:

What went wrong:

What I could do next time:

What I said:

My feelings:

The intention of my actions:

What went wrong:

What I could do next time:

What I said:

My feelings:

The intention of my actions:

What went wrong:

What I could do next time:

What words would you use to describe yourself?

What words would your friends use to describe you?

What identity traits do you actively lean into?

Do these traits ever cause you problems or get in your way?

What identity traits do you actively avoid or reject?

Could any aspects of of these "negative" traits be helpful to you?

What would a XYZ person do?

What strengths do you personality traits give you?

You might consider some of your personality traits as weaknesses, but in what way might they be viewed as strengths?

What abilities do these strengths give you?

What kind of person do you aspire to be?

If you were that kind of person, how might your thinking be different?

How might your actions be different?

*Try to use positive statements, rather than negative ones.
Eg: Instead of "I wouldn't make impulse purchases" try "I would be intentional in my buying habits."*

How could I become an XYZ person?

> Start with your last answer from the previous page:

What kind of actions would you be taking if you were an XYZ person?

If this was the way you lived your life, how would you think about things?

How would you describe yourself if you were that kind of person?

What are the strengths of being that kind of person?

Can you spot any signs (however small) of any of those strengths in yourself currently? Where do they show up? How could you practise using these strengths more?

It takes bravery to believe in yourself and your potential. It's OK if you find it difficult at first.

CHIRP goal setting

C Clear

H How will you know?

I Important

R Reasonable

P Period of time

Key Words

How will I feel?

Inspiring Quote

Copyright Chirp Ltd 2022 www.chirp-home.co.uk

Planning ladder

Goal	Goal
7	7
6	6
5	5
4	4
3	3
2	2
1	1

Time planning

1 Non-negotiable - Important and time sensitive

2 Schedule - Important but not time sensitive

3 The cherry on the cupcake - Optional and flexible

am ⟶ pm

Monday

Tuesday

Wednesday

Thursday

Friday

Saturday

Sunday

Daily planner

Type of routine:

Time	Activity

Procrastination

An instance when I have noticed myself procrastinating:

What thoughts am I having while I'm procrastinating?

Does this feel like overwhelm or underwhelm?

Which ideas from the previous pages resonate with me?

Try out some of the methods and record your experience:

The wiggly line of change

New behaviour:

Old behaviour:

What might have contributed to this "blip"?

What can I learn from this experience? What might I do differently next time?

A reminder of the progress I have already made:

My action plan for resetting and picking up where I left off:

Zoom in, zoom out

Zoom in

What is the over-all area or task?

What are the components of this area or task?

Pick one of these components. Break this down further into specifics.

Pick one of these specifics. What is your course of action for this thing individually?

What are you focussed on?

What category is this part of?

Where does this category sit compared to others?

How do you view this object in the wider context of your life?

Zoom out

Copyright Chirp Ltd 2022 www.chirp-home.co.uk

Letting go

Use this page to note down helpful and empowering thoughts you have when making decisions about letting objects go.
Come back here as a reminder if you get stuck in the future.

The flow of objects

What do I currently have too much of?

What would feel like the "right amount" of these items to me? (Quantity, volume etc)

What is my plan for removing unwanted items from my home? Where can I dispose of, recycle, donate, or sell?

My strategy for keeping on top of accumulation in the future:

Why is this important to me? How will I remind myself of this?

Weighing up a purchase

What is the item?

Why do I want it?

Would I still want it if it was full price? Will I still want it in a week's time if I don't buy it now?

What benefit would it bring me?

Will this item bring me this benefit on its own, or does it depend on other factors?

Are these other factors present, achieveable, or realistic?

Where will I keep it? Do I have space?

How often will I use it? Will I still be using it in a year's time? Are there options to borrow or rent it instead?

How will I dispose of it when I no longer need it? Can it be fixed if it breaks?

Stock control

Item	How long it lasts	Stock level	When to next buy

Overstock alert!
(don't buy this for a while)

Clutter-free gifting

Here are some prompts to help you to explain clutter-free gifting to friends and family.

This year I'm taking part in the Chirp Clutter-Free Gifting Challenge! This is all about reducing the amount of "stuff" given and received during celebrations, and bringing the focus back to connecting with the people who are important to us.

I'd love to try one of the following instead:

Spending time together:

....

....

Feeling connected:

....

....

Exploring a new experience:

....

....

Helping out:

....

....

Something else:

....

....

About the author

Amy Thompson is a declutter coach based in Sussex, UK. She works face to face and online with people overwhelmed with clutter and disorganisation in their homes.

A fascination with the way we interact with the spaces we inhabit led her to a career in Architecture and Interior design. After a life changing journey travelling around Japan, she founded Chirp to create home environments to help people thrive.

www.chirp-home.co.uk
IG: @chirp_ltd

Professional information:
- Diploma in Transformational Coaching - Animas Centre for Coaching (ICF accredited course).
- Member of APDO (The Association of Professional Declutterers and Organisers).
- Hoarding Awareness for Professional Practitioners – Hoarding Disorders UK CIC
- Neurodiversity, Executive Functions and Clutter – Hoarding Disorders UK CIC
- ADHD for Organisers – Free Your Space
- MA, Interior Design - University for the Creative Arts
- BA(Hons), Architecture - University for the Creative Arts

www.ingramcontent.com/pod-product-compliance
Lightning Source LLC
Chambersburg PA
CBHW070433010526
44118CB00014B/2029